THE
LITTLE EXOTIC
FRUIT BOOK

Susan Fleming

PIATKUS

Other titles in this series include:

The Little Green Avocado Book
The Little Garlic Book
The Little Pepper Book
The Little Lemon Book
The Little Strawberry Book
The Little Mushroom Book
The Little Bean Book
The Little Rice Book
The Little Tea Book
The Little Coffee Book
The Little Curry Book
The Little Chocolate Book
The Little Mediterranean Food Book
The Little Exotic Vegetable Book
The Little Yoghurt Book

First published in 1987
by Judy Piatkus (Publishers) Limited,
5 Windmill Street, London W1

British Library Cataloguing in Publication Data
Fleming, Susan
    The little exotic fruit book
    1. Cookery (Fruit)
    I. Title
    641.6′4   TX811

ISBN 0-86188-583-0

Drawings by Linda Broad
Designed by Sue Ryall
Cover illustrated by Lynne Robinson

Phototypeset in Linotron Plantin by
Phoenix Photosetting, Chatham
Printed and bound in Great Britain by
The Bath Press, Avon

CONTENTS

INTRODUCTION

During the last few years, thanks to new and improved transportation methods, many exotic fruits have become more common in Britain – on sale in ethnic shops, in the larger, better supermarkets, and sometimes even in the displays of more adventurous local greengrocers. If you've ever gazed open-mouthed at individual specimens, wondering what on earth they are, or what to do with them, then this little book should help.

It gives descriptions of the fruit, approximations of flavour and smell, details of preparation and ideas of how to eat and serve, as well as a few snippets of botanical, historical, nutritional, cosmetic and general interest. Because of space, many have had to be omitted – those fruit which are eaten principally as vegetables, for instance, like tomatoes, avocado, ackee and breadfruit. Olives, too, are a fruit, but they deserve a book of their own.

Exotics may be a little more expensive than our more familiar fruits, but in most cases only one or two are needed to lend their inimitable flavours or that sense of glamour to a dish or meal. An ordinary fruit salad will be transformed by a few cubes of mango, sizzling green slices of kiwifruit or some carambola stars; a simple whipped cream garnish can be elevated to the heights of fragrant luxury by the inclusion of the flesh of half a passion fruit.

Treat exotics as simply as you can in order to appreciate them at their succulent best – eating them as a fruit out of hand, or puréeing them raw to add to mousses, icecreams, sweet soufflés or fools, or to make a sauce. There can be no better breakfast, for instance, than a half papaya sprinkled with lime juice, and no more delicious after-meal treat than a couple of slices of fresh, ripe and juicy pineapple or a bowlful of freshly peeled lychees. Cook them only rarely for that special occasion, or to preserve their uniqueness in jams, jellies and chutneys.

Handle all of these fruits with care, prepare and eat them simply, and bring an exotic flavour into your life!

CAPE GOOSEBERRY
Physalis peruviana

These fruits belong to the genus Physalis, which belongs in turn to the Solanaceae family – including such varying relations as potatoes, tomatoes, tobacco and deadly nightshade! Fortunately, most physalis are edible, even those more familiarly used in dried flower arrangements. Originally from Peru, Cape gooseberry bushes became an important fruit commercially in the Cape of Good Hope at the beginning of the 19th century, thus their most common name. They are also known as 'Golden Berries' (in cans and on seed packets).

The golden-orange berries, which have good amounts of Vitamins A and B, are cherry size and are completely encased in a loose, straw-coloured, papery calyx to protect against insects and bruising. Green berries are unripe. The myriad seeds are edible and the flavour is sharp and sweet, like unripe blackcurrants.

Cape gooseberries are most easily and pleasurably eaten raw out of the calyx: fold the natural papery divisions back and use as a handle. The berries are also commonly dipped in liqueur-flavoured fondant or caramel and served as *petits-fours*. They can be stewed, made into jams, compotes, fruit cheeses and put into tarts, and in South Africa they are used as the basis of a summer pudding.

EXOTIC FRUIT PETITS FOURS

You can make the fondant yourself – any good general cookery book will have a recipe – or buy it already prepared in packets. Cape gooseberries are the best choice, but kumquats, stoned dates, lychees and rambutans could also be tried, as could well-dried carambola slices or pineapple chunks. Prepare on the day you want to serve them as juices can seep through and ruin the fondant.

8 oz (225g) fondant
20 Cape gooseberries (or a variety of fruits)
about 3 tablespoons water (or half water, half rum)

Break the fondant up into small pieces (if you are using the packet variety), and put into a bowl over a pan of simmering water. Add the water or water and rum and stir until the fondant is a smooth coating consistency. Fold back the calyxes of the berries carefully and dip the berries into the fondant so that they are covered. Hold over the bowl until the fondant sets, then place in a small paper case. Repeat with the remainder. (Other fruits do not have a natural 'handle', so use a wooden skewer for dipping.)

4

CARAMBOLA
Averrhoa carambola

Carambolas are the prolific fruit of a small tree, native to Indonesia and Malaysia, now grown in many other countries. Small quantities are occasionally available in the United Kingdom throughout the year. Carambolas are also known as 'Star Fruit' and 'Star Apples'.

Carambolas are generally about 3–5 inches (7.5–12.5cm) long (occasionally very much larger in Chinese grocers). They are waxy and yellow-green and have five ribs along the length of the fruit which, when sliced across, give perfect stars. The skin is edible, but the tough edges may need to be trimmed. Remove seeds from the slices. The flavour of the yellow-orange flesh is crisp, cool and astringent, like a sweet lemon.

Carambolas contain oxalic acid (like spinach, sorrel and rhubarb) which inhibits the body's absorption of calcium and iron.

As the shape of the slices is so attractive, carambolas are best used simply, raw in fruit or vegetable salads, or as a garnish for both savoury and sweet main courses – a poached salmon looks magnificent with a central spine of stars. These stars are candied or crystallised in India.

5

CITRUS FRUITS
Citrus spp

The genus *Citrus* includes many fruit so familiar nowadays that it is difficult to remember their 'exotic' origins: they are all the fruit of small trees or shrubs, grown mostly in the tropics, often now in warm temperate regions such as southern Europe. They include sweet and bitter (or Seville) oranges, the tangerine or mandarin (and all the other loose-skinned citrus varieties such as clementine and satsuma), the grapefruit and lemon. There are a number of hybrids which are becoming popular, including the ortanique (probably a cross between the orange and tangerine). These below are perhaps less familiar, more justifiably 'exotic'.

The CITRON (*C. medica*) is closely related to the lemon, but is larger, more warty, and more like a quince in shape. It was probably the first citrus fruit to reach Europe, and was thought to have been cultivated in the Hanging Gardens of Babylon. The flesh is meagre and too bitter for eating; it is the thick skin that is used primarily for candied peel.

The POMELO or SHADDOCK (*C. grandis*), the largest of the citrus fruit, is probably the ancestor of the grapefruit (thought to be a hybrid of the pomelo and the orange). It originated in South-East Asia, and was later 'transplanted' to the Caribbean by a Captain Shaddock, hence its other common name. It looks like an enormous grapefruit, with very thick yellow-green rind. The white, occasionally pink, flesh is dry but the flavour is pleasant, and it may be used in the same way as grapefruit.

The UGLI FRUIT (*C. reticulata*) is a variety of tangelo (tangerine × orange × grapefruit hybrids) and it was first discovered growing wild 70 years ago by a Jamaican plantation owner. It is large and has a misshapen and ugly look to it, hence its unjustifiably disparaging name. The thick knobbly skin is orange-green, and the flesh is sweet and juicy, a combination of all the qualities of its parents. Eat and use as an orange or grapefruit. It is available in the UK from December to April, chiefly from Jamaica.

The LIME (*C. aurantifolia*) is a small sour fruit closely related to the lemon, and can be used in many of the same ways. The skin is usually green, and it is thin, so handle limes with care. There are several varieties, but all have a tangy, sharp, spicy flavour. Use them for juice instead of lemon in salad dressings, to prevent discoloration of certain fruits, sprinkled on a breakfast papaya – or to make lime curd or the famous Florida Key Lime Pie. Raw fish is 'cooked' by marination in lime juice in the South American *ceviche*, and limes make hot pickles in India.

All citrus fruits are a major source of Vitamin C – lime juice was added to the grog of sailors to prevent scurvy, the C deficiency disease, thus the name 'limeys'. Gum health is also related to C.

UGLI DUCKLING

Instead of the more classic orange, this duck recipe uses succulent slices of ugli fruit, and makes a delicious dish with a name that's difficult to resist!

1 × 4–4½ lb (1.82–2 kg) duck
salt
1 medium ugli fruit
4 tablespoons Cointreau
1 small bunch watercress

Prick the duck all over with a fork. Rub a little salt into the skin and place on a rack or trivet in a roasting pan. Roast for 1½–1¾ hours in a preheated oven at 350°F/180°C/Gas 4, without basting.

Meanwhile, cut the skin and pith off the ugli fruit. Carefully slice the fruit and then cut each slice in half. Poach the slices gently in the Cointreau for 4–5 minutes.

Portion the duck and place on individual warmed serving plates. Pour the delicious juices over each portion, and garnish with the ugli fruit slices and some fresh watercress.

Serves 3–4

LIME AND MANGO SHERBET

1 large ripe mango
2 tablespoons fresh lime juice
1/4 pint (150 ml) soured cream
2 egg whites
2 oz (50 g) caster sugar
slices of lime, to decorate

Slice the mango over a bowl to catch all juice and then scrape the flesh from the skin and off the stone. Put flesh and juice into a processor or liquidiser goblet, along with the lime juice and cream. Blend to a purée then return to the bowl.

In another bowl, whip the egg whites until they hold soft peaks. Add the sugar, 1 teaspoon at a time, beating continuously. Fold the egg whites into the mango and lime mixture and transfer to a freezer container. Freeze until firm, and serve in chilled glasses decorated with lime slices.

Serves 4–6

CUSTARD APPLES
Annona spp

The fruits of small trees and shrubs of the Annona family, native to the American tropics, are often known collectively as custard apples – because of the custard-like texture of many. It is a useful family, one annona being the source of Guinea pepper, once imported to Europe as a substitute for real pepper, others giving a nutmeg alternative and Macassar oil (to counter which antimacassars were necessary). They are multiple fruits, developing in divisions, each with its own (inedible) seed.

The CUSTARD APPLE (*A. squamosa*, 'full of scales') is also known as sweetsop and sugar apple, and is the most commonly seen. It looks rather like an oval or pear-shaped armadillo, yellow-green, and can weigh up to 4½ lb (2 kg). The flesh is white and tastes like banana- or strawberry-scented clotted cream.

The CHERIMOYA (*A. cherimolia*) was first grown by the Incas (from whose language is derived the name), and is a little larger than the sweetsop. It is green-skinned and scaly with a firm white flesh and a taste reminiscent of pineapple.

The SOURSOP (*A. muricata*, 'rough, with hard points') is most common in the West Indies. It is the largest of the annonas, oval or heart-shaped, green with rows of spines, and can weigh up to about 8 lb (3.5 kg). It is the least sweet, with a white fibrous flesh compared by some to blackcurrants, by others to a cross between strawberries, pineapples and cinnamon.

The BULLOCK'S HEART or RAMPHAL (*A. reticulata*, 'with a net-like pattern'), was a fruit offered to Columbus when he reached the New World. It is slightly larger than the sweetsop, has a round or heart shape, red or brown skin, and a more solid granular texture. The flavour of the yellowish flesh is less aromatic than the other annonas, slightly reminiscent of pears and cinnamon.

The ATEMOYA (*A. atemoya*) is a cross between *A. squamosa* and *A. cherimolia* and is cultivated in Israel and Florida.

Annonas should be bought and eaten when ripe and soft, but firm fruit can be ripened at home in the dark. Many contain Vitamins B and C and some minerals such as iron. To eat, cut fruit in half and spoon the flesh out. Eat as it is, discarding the seeds, or sieve and use as a 'custard sauce', or mix with cream for a fool, mousse, soufflé or icecream – soursop icecream is a West Indian speciality. The flesh is often used in drinks, both soft and alcoholic.

DATE
Phoenix dactylifera

The date palm is native to the Middle East, and the date is one of the world's oldest known fruits: wild date stones have been discovered in Palaeolithic caves (some 50,000 years old). They are cultivated commercially in North Africa, India, California, Israel – and Alicante in southern Spain, the only part of Europe where the palms will fruit.

Smooth, brown and shiny fresh dates are now available throughout the year in the UK, coming mainly from Israel. To remove the single grooved seed or stone, cut date in half, or push stone straight through the length with a skewer; to remove the papery skin, squeeze from one end and the flesh will pop out the other.

The main constituent of dates is sugar carbohydrate, about 60–70%, but they also contain some vitamins and minerals. They are thought to be aphrodisiac, and were certainly known as a laxative by Apicius – to ensure an 'easy passage', he advised using 'a dozen scruples of plump dates'!

Dates can be eaten just as they are raw or, popularly, stuffed with marzipan, nuts or cream cheese. They are very sweet, so are good fresh fruit salads, can be chopped and added to mueslis, to vegetable salads (with carrots and raisins, say), and are delicious with yoghurt. They can also be cooked in cakes, loaves and confectionary, as a stuffing for meats, and as an ingredient in Moroccan fruit tajines or stews.

FRESH DATES IN SYRUP

These dates – from Iraq – can be served as a nutritious sweetmeat or in small bowls with a spoon.

2 lb (900 g) fresh dates
1 pint (600 ml) water
10 oz (300 g) granulated sugar
whole cloves
a few drops of lemon juice
blanched almonds (or walnut halves)

Carefully peel the dates, then boil them in the water until tender. Drain and dry the dates thoroughly, retaining the water, then push out the stones (or slit through the sides). Place a layer of sugar in a heavy based pan, then cover with dates and a few cloves; repeat layers until sugar and dates are used up. Leave overnight then remove dates, shaking off the sugar.

Add the date cooking water to the sugar and cloves in the pan and boil to reduce to a thick syrup. Put one almond inside each date, and place the dates in the syrup. Boil gently for 10 minutes then leave to cool. Pack the dates into clean glass jars, then pour the syrup over them.

DURIAN
Durio zibethinus

The durian tree is native to Malaysia and has been cultivated there and in Indonesia and Thailand for hundreds of years. The durian belongs to the Bombacaceae family, and related trees are the bao-bob, balsa and kapok. The Latin name *zibethinus* derives from the Arab word for a civet cat, a notoriously ill-smelling creature, and the comparison is perhaps elucidated by this 'limerick' (first published in *Horticultural Science*, 9, 1973, and quoted in *Tropical Fruits* by J.A. Samson):

> The durian – neither Wallace nor Darwin agreed on it.
> Darwin said: 'May your worst enemies be forced to feed on it.'
> Wallace cried, 'It's delicious.'
> Darwin replied, 'I'm suspicious,
> For the flavour is scented like papaya fermented, after a fruit-eating bat has pee'd on it.'

For the durian must be the most controversial of fruits. It is large, brownish yellow-green, and covered with thick hard spikes. Its smell has been likened to stale vomit or to custard passed through sewage, and it is so penetrating that many Asian airlines have specifically forbidden passengers to carry them. This odour is said to be least strong just as the fruits drop, but as they can weigh up to 10 lb (4.5 kg) a wait beneath the tree could be a dangerous

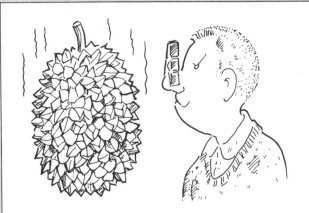

occupation (indeed many locals in the tropics, to make sure of their catch, and to prevent their delectation by equally enthusiastic monkeys and elephants, spend nights *in* the tree).

The taste of durian, however, is nectar to aficionados, rich and aromatic, with one commentator likening it to a 'mixture of full flavoured cheese, mingled with peanuts, pineapple and apricots, a little garlic and a dash of sherry.'

Inside the spines is a soft custard-like flesh divided into 4-5 segments, each filled with seeds (these are chestnut size and can be roasted and eaten like chestnuts). The pulp can range from creamy pale yellow to bright orange. It is usually eaten fresh – very occasionally available in the UK from ethnic shops, in winter and summer – and it is also canned and dried.

FIG
Ficus carica

The many varieties of fig trees are probably native to Western Asia. They were revered by the Ancient Greeks, Romans (fig seeds have been identified among Roman remains in Britain), and Egyptians (who left baskets of the fruit in their tombs, and used the hard wood of the mulberry fig for sarcophagi). Figs are mentioned in the Bible, and were presumably grown in the Garden of Eden!

Supplies to the UK come mainly from Mediterranean countries, although figs can be grown in Britain. Near Worthing in Sussex, fig orchards established by the mid-18th century were still producing fruit in 1904. And trees in sheltered London gardens – and outside the National Gallery – bear delicious fruits. In Britain, figs are parthenocarpic (they are able to fruit without being pollinated), but the best eating variety, Smyrna, require pollination by the female fig wasp which breeds in the wild caprifigs. When Smyrna figs were introduced to California in the 19th century, wild caprifigs and wasps had to be introduced as well.

Fresh figs – normally green, black or purple-red with a bloom – are available from early summer to autumn. They are ready when soft, and should be eaten as soon as possible. Inside the skin is the flower of the tree, and this 'flesh' is soft, red, sweet and fibrous with lots of tiny seeds. Dried figs – with a 50% sugar content – are available all year round – the most famous varieties being the Smyrna from Turkey, the Black Mission from America and the Calimyrna, a hybrid of a native Californian variety and Smyrna.

Figs are best known for their mild laxative properties (syrup of figs is still included in the British Pharmaceutical Codex). Culpeper, however, amidst his many fig cures – for warts, leprosy and the falling sickness – did not include constipation. Figs contain Vitamins A and C, and calcium, iron and potassium. In folk medicine, because of an enzyme similar to that of papaya and pineapple, they are used to bring down swellings and to reduce puffiness under the eyes.

Figs are most delicious eaten raw as a dessert with cream. Peel only if skin is tough. They can be stuffed, served as a breakfast fruit, or as a starter with Parma ham. They can be poached in syrup or alcohol – gently, so that they retain that wonderful shape – and they can be made into jams. Apicius preserved figs in honey – and also, less honourably, force-fed his pigs with figs and mead to improve the flavour of the meat, and to expand the liver for an early *foie gras*. Dried figs are used in baked cakes and pudding, and in confectionary in the Middle East.

SLICED FIGS WITH RASPBERRY SAUCE

This sauce – which can be spiked with a little raspberry liqueur – can be used as a colourful base for many other exotic fruits or for a mixed fruit salad (try papaya, mango and kiwifruit).

8 ripe purple figs
12 oz (350 g) raspberries
5 oz (150 g) icing sugar
juice of 1 lemon
¼ pint (150 ml) double cream, chilled

Peel the figs carefully and cut each into 6 pieces. Liquidise half the raspberries and then pass through a fine sieve. Add the icing sugar and lemon juice to the purée and mix. Pour a puddle of the sauce on to individual serving plates and then arrange 12 fig pieces decoratively on top. Chill until needed, then whip the cream, pipe on to the plates, and decorate with the remaining raspberries.

Serves 4

GUAVA
Psidium guajava

Guavas are the fruits of tropical trees of the myrtle family (therefore related to the clove, pimento or allspice and eucalyptus trees, as well as the pineapple guava, the feijoa). They are native to Central America (believed to have been first brought to Europe by the conquering Spaniards), but are now grown all over the world in warm climates. The name *guava* is an adaptation of that learned by Columbus from the Arawak Indians in the West Indies; and *psidium* comes from the Greek for pomegranate (probably because of the many small seeds in the fruit). Guavas are among the most successful and fast-growing fruit trees, but they have become a pest in many areas: in Hawaii the guava is considered to be as much of a danger to indigenous plants as the cutting back of forests for the ever-burgeoning tourist industry; and in the Fiji Islands it has been classified as a 'noxious weed'. Supplies to the UK come from Brazil, South Africa and the West Indies, most commonly in the latter half of the year.

There are some 150 species of guava, the commonest of which is the Lemon Guava. Yellowish-green in colour, it is a round or pear-shaped fruit about the size of a small apple. The main characteristic of any guava, whatever its type, is the strong musky smell which is, it must be said, undeniably like that left after a tom-cat has marked his territory. Inside the thin skin, the flesh is divided into two distinct areas: a shell next to the skin which contains the flavour, and a pulpy middle which contains the seeds. Shell, pulp and seeds are all edible. The colour of the flesh ranges from white to pink, the texture is somewhat like under-ripe pears, and the flavour is sweet but tart and aromatic. Store guavas apart from other fruit, and eat when the skin gives to gentle pressure.

Guavas are of great nutritional value because of their exceptionally high content of Vitamin C, many times that of citrus fruit.

Guavas can be cut in half and the flesh eaten out of the skin with a spoon, or they can be peeled and used in fruit salads. A few slices add flavour to apple pies or sauces, and they can be cooked in a light syrup and sieved for use in mousses, icecreams, jams and jellies. A canned guava jam was imported into the UK during the last war from South Africa; a guava paste is exported all over the world from the Caribbean; whole guavas are canned, as are the shells.

GUAVA JELLY

Eat as a jelly on bread, or serve with venison or roast pork. For a medlar jelly, add ½ inch (1.25 cm) stick of cinnamon and the rind and juice of 1 lemon when simmering. For a quince jelly, add some bruised allspice berries while simmering.

4 lb (1.8 kg) ripe guavas, wiped and sliced (do no peel)
water
sugar

Put the guava slices into a preserving pan and pour in just enough water to cover. Simmer until the fruit is very soft. Strain through a jelly bag or doubled muslin for at least 12 hours. Do not squeeze. Discard the pulp.

Measure the juice, and for each 1 pint (600 ml) water, add 12 oz (350 g) warmed sugar. Heat until the sugar has dissolved and then boil hard until setting point is reached – about 10–15 minutes. Leave to cool, then pour into clean jars and cover. Store in a cool dark place.

Makes about 4 lb (1.8 kg)

KIWIFRUIT
Actinidia chinensis

Although the kiwifruit has, in the last few years, become almost as familiar as peaches and pineapples, its origins and botanical family is a little uncertain. Seeds of the Chinese gooseberry – as it was first known – were brought to New Zealand from the Yangtse Valley in China in 1906. After an initial show of faith and many trials, the vines established themselves in the central part of North Island, and the New Zealand Chinese gooseberry industry was born. During the 1950s, export possibilities began to be explored, and an America which was at that time wary of anything even remotely 'eastern', suggested an alternative name might be the answer. The first rejected suggestion was 'Melonette', but then the importers came up with 'Kiwifruit', naming it after New Zealand's national bird. In the 1970s the sales of kiwifruit took off and, as one expert has remarked, it has become 'almost the badge of the *nouvelle cuisine*'. Main supplies to the UK come from New Zealand from June to January, but other countries are now cultivating kiwifruit – France, Italy, Israel and the USA – and they are available all year round.

The fruit is duck-egg sized, with a furry brown skin (thus the French call them *souris végétales* or vegetable mice). Inside the skin the flesh is a vivid green with radiating spokes of tiny black edible seeds. The flavour is tangy and refreshing and can be reminiscent of strawberries, gooseberries, melons, grapes or bananas. Many people experience a slightly cloying aftertaste.

One of the principal joys of kiwifruit is that they store well – if kept cool, for up to six months. To delay ripening, store them apart from the ripening effects of the ethylene gas of other fruits like bananas, apples and pears; if speedy ripening is required, place kiwis in a plastic bag in company with one of those fruits.

Kiwifruit are rich in Vitamins C and E – twice that of a medium orange and an avocado respectively. They also contain dietary fibre, potassium, folic acid and chromium. The enzyme, actinidin, which acts as a meat tenderizer (place inner skin or puréed flesh over meat), prevents gelatine from setting so a vegetable alternative like agar agar should be used in soufflés and jellies, etc.

Kiwifruit are undeniably best when eaten raw. Cut them in half and spoon the flesh out of the skin, or peel them and use thin slices as colourful garnishes for fruit or vegetable salads, for muesli, for selected meat, poultry or fish dishes, and, of course, for puddings. Kiwifruit slices are almost traditional now in the best Antipodean pavlova. Kiwi can also be made into icecreams, jams and pickles – the latter cooling as a sambal with hot curries.

NEW ZEALAND KIWIFRUIT MOUSSE

An ideal starter for a summer dinner party.

4 kiwifruit
2 oz (50 g) full-fat soft cream cheese
½ level teaspoon paprika
freshly ground black pepper
1 tablespoon lemon juice
1 teaspoon white wine vinegar
4 tablespoons vegetable oil
salt

Remove both ends of each kiwifruit with a sharp knife. Do not peel. Using an apple corer carefully remove the centre of each fruit and reserve.

Mix together the cheese, paprika and black pepper to taste. Fill the hollowed centres of the fruit with the cheese mixture. Chill.

Chop the reserved fruit cores finely. Add the lemon juice, white wine vinegar and oil. Mix well and season to taste.

Peel the filled kiwifruit carefully, and cut into four slices widthwise. Arrange on individual plates over a quarter of the kiwifruit dressing. Serve chilled.

Serves 4

Exotic Fruit Pavlova

4 egg whites
8 oz (225 g) caster sugar
2 teaspoons cornflour
1 teaspoon white wine vinegar
½ pint (300 ml) double cream
2 passion fruit, halved
3 kiwifruit, peeled and sliced

Whip the egg whites until stiff, and gradually add the sugar, beating until smooth. Whisk in cornflour and vinegar. Pile on to a baking sheet lined with oiled and sugar-dusted foil, and hollow it in the centre. Bake for 1½ hours in a very cool oven, preheated to 250°F/120°C/Gas ½, until firm on the outside (but like marshmallow within). Remove to a serving plate and cool.

Whip the cream in a basin then mix in the passion fruit pulp. Pile this speckled fragrant cream into the pavlova shell and arrange the slices of kiwifruit on top.

Serves 4–6

KUMQUAT
Fortunella japonica

Native to China (despite the botanical name), kumquats are very closely related to citrus fruits but have a greater resistance to cold, enabling them to be grown much further north. They are now cultivated in many countries, among them Brazil, Malaysia, France, Israel, Africa, Australia, Morocco and America. Their name comes from the Cantonese *kam kwat* or 'gold orange'; *fortunella* is for Robert Fortune, a nineteenth-century Scots horticulturist who collected in China. Hybrids include the limequat and the orangequat. A related variety is the calamondin which grows in America and the Philippines.

Kumquats look like round or oval oranges, dimpled skin and all, but are only about 2 inches (5 cm) across. The flesh, rinds and seeds (if any) are all edible. The flavour is tangy sour-sweet, aromatic, a combination of several citrus elements. Kumquats should be bright orange, shiny and smooth, but any greenness will ripen at home. Store in the refrigerator for about a week.

Kumquats, like their citrus relatives, are a good source of Vitamin C. At Chinese New Year, pots of trees bearing the golden fruit brighten every home with the promise of prosperity in the year to come.

Eat the raw fruit whole, or slice for fruit salads or garnishes (good with duck, pork, or those decorative slices on a pâté). They can also be dipped into fondant like Cape gooseberries for *petits-fours* (see page 4). They are most commonly candied, pickled or, although not technically a citrus fruit, made into marmalade. They can be stewed in syrup for a dessert or used as a pie filling.

PICKLED KUMQUATS

An unusual 'pickle' to serve with game, or for a ploughman's lunch with a difference.

1 lb (450 g) kumquats
1 pint (600 ml) preserving vinegar
2 oz (50 g) soft brown sugar
12 whole cloves
15 black peppercorns

Wash the kumquats briefly and dry them well. Pierce each a couple of times with a knitting needle, then put into a clean preserving jar. Bring the remaining ingredients to the boil and simmer for 10 minutes. Cool slightly and then pour over the kumquats. When cold, seal with greaseproof paper and a lid, and keep for at least a month before using.

LOQUAT
Eriobotrya japonica

The loquat, also known as Japanese medlar, is native to China and south Japan and belongs to the Rosaceae family, along with most temperate fruits such as apples. Indeed, it is the only member which can grow (at a height) in the tropics and subtropics. The tree is evergreen and was first introduced to the Mediterranean by the French in 1874, and to hothouses at Kew earlier, in 1787. It grows wild in many Mediterranean countries, and it is under cultivation also in India, North Africa, Australia, California and Florida. The name loquat is an adaptation of the Cantonese *lu-kywit*, referring to the orange colour of the fruit; the Greek *eriobotrya* refers to the woolly, downy appearance of the fruit skin (usually rubbed off by the time the fruit reaches Britain).

About the size of plums or crab apples, loquats are yellow-orange in colour. They do not travel particularly well and are often bruised. The skin can be eaten although it is quite tough in comparison with the white to yellow flesh, soft and pear-like in texture. The flavour is sweet-acid and pleasant. There are from one to five large, inedible, shiny brown stones in a cluster.

Loquats can be eaten raw on their own or in fruit salads, but they can also be lightly poached in syrup, then sieved to use in a tart or mousse. They can be candied, spiced or made into a savoury sauce. As they are high in pectin, they make good jams and jellies. In Bermuda, loquats are used to make a liqueur, and they can be marinated to made a delicious fruit flavoured gin or brandy. Loquats are available canned in syrup in Chinese supermarkets.

Here is a curious story about loquats. It is believed by both the British and Spanish that when the apes leave the Rock of Gibraltar, the British too will leave. When in 1914 the number of ape females had been reduced to three, London became alarmed. The Royal Regiment of Artillery was ordered to cherish the remainder, and was offered a grant to buy them olives, locust beans and green figs – but not loquats, which made them vomit!

LYCHEE
Litchi chinensis

Lychees are native to sub-tropical areas of South China and have been cultivated there for at least 2,000 years. Lychees belong to the Sapindaceae, the soapberry family, and related fruits are rambutan, logan and pulasan. Lychees are now cultivated widely – in Madagascar, South Africa, Mauritius, Israel, South-East Asia, Australia, New Zealand and America – and are available in Britain throughout most of the year, especially at Christmas when their tart sweetness is a good antidote to seasonal excess. In southern China, every village has its *li chi* trees, and the season runs only from May or June to August, although there is one variety – its name translating literally as 'third moon red' – that ripens earlier. The longan (*lung-an*, dragon's eye), although smaller with less flesh, enjoys a popularity there because its fruits continue to please after the lychee season is over.

Lychees are small plum size, with a thin, brittle and scaly brown-red casing which encloses pearly white translucent flesh. This in turn hugs a hard brown inedible seed. Lychees are often available on the branch in clusters as they keep better that way. The texture of the flesh is jelly-like, dry at first, becoming juicy, and the flavour is rather like a scented grape. Lychees are also canned, their flavour retained more successfully than most other fruits, and they are occasionally available dried, when they are known as Chinese nuts, and taste rather like raisins.

Lychees contain natural sugar and good quantities of Vitamin C. They are used in Chinese folk medicine as a general tonic, as are other 'gelatinous' foods such as shark's fin and birds' nests.

Lychees are the best dessert after Chinese food (canned in most restaurants). They can be served with cream, mixed into fruit salads, made into ice-creams and sorbets, or poached in syrup to be served cold. They can also be used in some Chinese stir-fry dishes or sweet and sour sauces.

FISH WITH LYCHEES

Use lemon sole or plaice for a classic dish with a
Chinese accent.

6 fish, filleted and skinned (keep heads, skin and bones)
juice of 1 lemon
1/4 bottle dry white wine
9 fresh lychees
1 oz (25 g) butter
2 tablespoons plain flour
1/4 pint (150 ml) double cream

For the fish stock:
1 medium onion, peeled
3 parsley stalks
1 bayleaf
8 black peppercorns
1 teaspoon salt

Roll the fillets, skinned sides inwards, and pack into
a buttered ovenproof dish. Pour the lemon juice
over them and set aside.

Make a fish stock with the fish trimmings, onion,
herbs, peppercorns and salt and enough water to
cover. Bring to the boil, simmer for about 30
minutes, then strain.

Pour the wine over the fish and add enough stock
to come halfway up the fillets. Cover the dish
with foil and bake in a preheated oven at
350°F/180°C/Gas 4 for 15–20 minutes. Meanwhile,
peel, pit and quarter the lychees.

Pour the liquid from the fish into a saucepan, and

scatter the lychees over the fish. Re-cover the dish and keep warm.

Boil the liquid until it reduces to about ½ pint (300 ml). Melt the butter in a clean pan, add the flour and cook for a minute, stirring. Add the reduced liquid to make a sauce, stirring until it thickens. Add the cream, warm through, and pour over the fish and lychees.

Seves 6

MANGO
Mangifera indica

The 'king of fruits' is believed to have been culti-vated for over 4,000 years in India (still the world's largest producer), and Indian folklore and religious ceremonies are still closely linked with the tree – Buddha himself was said to have been presented with a mango grove under the shade of which he could find peace (although that heavy shade also provides an ideal habitat for mosquitoes).

Mangoes are now grown in most tropical climates, and imports to the UK all year round come from India, Egypt, East and West Africa, South America, the Philippines, Israel and the Caribbean.

The tree is a member of the Anacardiaceae family, along with the cashew and pistachio nut trees. Close relatives are trees which produce types of tannin and turpentine, the latter an epithet applied to the taste of many inferior mangoes! Interestingly, mango wood was once used for the crates in which opium was transported from India to China in the early nineteenth century.

Mangoes vary considerably in size, colour and shape, according to variety and country of origin. They can be round, heart- or kidney-shaped, and vary in colour from green (small and unripe, to be used for chutneys), to red, orange or yellow. They are ready for eating when soft to the touch. If bought unripe, wrap them in newspaper and keep in a warm place (the kitchen) until ripe. Store thereafter in the fridge. Mangoes are also available canned in slices or as purée, dried in slices, or as juice.

Mangoes are highly nutritious, being a major source of Vitamin A with some B and C. They are laxative and can cause unhappiness if eaten in excess. Every year, on one West Indian island, the hospital swells with groaning children – and adults – who have plucked the local trees too early and too much!

To eat the fruit, cut close to the large narrow stone along the length of the fruit on either side. Scoop the flesh out with a spoon from the skin sides, or make criss-cross cuts and turn the skin inside out to make a hedgehog shape. Don't forget to peel the central slice and nibble the flesh off the stone. The fruit can be peeled whole. Mangoes should really be eaten as simply as possible – raw as a dessert fruit (provide finger bowls, or have a bath afterwards as one writer has suggested), or in a fruit salad. Raw slices or nuggets can make a good accompaniment to cooked cold duck or chicken, and the flesh can be puréed for use in mousses, icecream or sorbets. Unripe and pectin-rich, green mangoes (which contain the most Vitamin C) make the best pickles and chutneys (see page 44) to accompany curries. *Amchoor* is a curry souring agent made from unripe mangoes.

CHICKEN WITH MANGO

Delicately flavoured, this should be accompanied by plain rice and a Chinese vegetable dish.

4 chicken breasts, skinned and boned
2 medium, firm mangoes, peeled and stoned
1 dessertspoon vegetable oil
2 large garlic cloves, peeled and finely chopped
1 inch (2.5 cm) fresh root ginger, peeled and finely chopped
2 tablespoons oyster sauce (available in good supermarkets and Chinese grocers)

Cut both the chicken breasts and the mangoes, separately, into bite-size strips. Heat the oil in a heavy frying pan or wok and add the garlic and ginger.

Sauté until just starting to turn colour. Add the chicken and stir-fry over a high heat, stirring constantly, until all the pieces are sealed. Reduce heat and stir in the oyster sauce. Lastly, fold in the mango pieces very carefully. When just heated through, serve immediately.

Serves 4

EXOTIC FRUIT DRINK

Similar drinks could be made with the flesh of many fruits – try pineapple, passion fruit, or babaco. You could also use less liquid and add ice cubes instead. These are processed with the fruit to make a crushed ice fruit cocktail: serve in tall glasses with all the trimmings.

1 mango, peeled, stoned and chopped
orange or apple juice, or bottled water
clear honey (optional)

Measure the volume of the mango flesh in a cup and then measure out the same volume of liquid. Work together in a blender or liquidiser until smooth. Add about 1 teaspoon honey if liked.

MANGOSTEEN
Garcinia mangostana

The mangosteen is one of the best fruits in the world. Although the tree is quite extensively cultivated in Indonesia and Malaysia, cultivation elsewhere is intermittent, as are supplies to Britain, probably due to the difficulties of propagation – the seed does not germinate well – and to the slowness of its growth, up to 15 years from seed to fruit. What supplies there are come from Java, Thailand and the West Indies as well as Asia. A close relation is *G. indica*, which produces the *kokum* used as a souring agent in Indian cookery.

The fruit on the tree looks uninspiring, round like an apple with a thick brownish-maroon crust or rind and several brown-green sepals around the stalk. Inside, though, the flesh, divided into lobes, is a pure translucent white, reminiscent of lychee, sitting in a cup of pink. Buy large fruit and twist or cut open at its widest point. Do this before the rind becomes too hard with age. (Watch your clothes as the tannic juices of the rind can stain – and they can also affect the flesh.) The texture is like lychee and the flavour – slightly acid, but delicious – has a touch of lychee intermingled with grape and apricot.

Remove the flesh from the rind as above and eat raw as a dessert fruit.

MEDLAR
Mespilus germanica

The medlar, perhaps more of a forgotten than an exotic fruit, is thought to have originated in southern Central Europe. It was highly prized in the Middle Ages – Chaucer's Reeve referred to it – and later, in the mid-16th century, the botanist William Turner recorded that medlar trees were common in England. Cultivated and appreciated until Victorian times, trees are now rare. The medlar is from the Rosaceae family, and so is related to apples, pears, loquats (Japanese medlars) and quinces. Fruits are occasionally available, from local wild or garden trees, or from Italy where the Naples medlar or azarole (fruit of a hawthorn) is also cultivated.

The medlar is like a small apple with a russet skin and a calyx in which the five seed vessels are all quite conspicuous – a botanical curiosity which led to the fruit being called 'openarse' until the more polite French name took over! The fruits are rock hard and have to be stored for some weeks until soft or 'bletted': 'they are kept in moist bran for a fortnight before being rotten enough to eat' (*Child's Guide*, 1850). The flesh, as might be expected, is then very soft, brown and granular, and the flavour is acidly aromatic and winey, which introduces its most popular usage: as a 'worthy mate for the best of liquors', especially claret or port.

Culpeper makes many claims for the medlar's efficacy in pregnancy: it prevents miscarriage and 'stayeth their longing after unusual meats'. It is also known in folk medicine as a counter to diarrhoea.

Very ripe medlars can be eaten from the skin with a spoon, or the flesh can be scraped out and mixed with cream and brown sugar. They can be baked with butter and cloves like apples, and Apicius mixed the sieved flesh with calf's or pork brains and eggs to make a huge omelette-like dish. Medlars make a jelly or fruit cheese to eat as a sweet or to serve with game (see page 21).

MEDLAR FOOL

1½lb (675 g) ripe medlars
2 tablespoons sherry
4 oz (100 g) soft brown sugar
¼ pint (150 ml) double cream
1 tablespoon toasted hazelnuts, chopped

Spoon the flesh carefully from the ripe medlars into a plastic sieve set over a bowl. Press through for a smooth purée. Stir in the sherry and the sugar. Whip the cream lightly – it should not be too stiff – and fold it into the purée. Spoon into glasses and chill for about 2½ hours. Just before serving, garnish with the toasted hazelnuts.

Serves 4–6

PASSION FRUIT
Passiflora edulis

Although many fruit eaters are indeed passionate about it, the passion fruit (or purple granadilla) was in fact named by Spanish priests in the early 17th century. They compared the convolutions of the glorious flower to Christ's Passion – the crown of thorns, the nails, the wounds, and the ten faithful apostles.

Originally native to Brazil, the climbing vines of the Passiflora family – about 350 of them – are now widely planted in the tropics, but can also be grown in some Mediterranean countries. Supplies to the UK all year round come from Kenya, the West Indies, Brazil, Israel and Spain. A related fruit is the giant granadilla (*P. quadrangularis*).

The most common passion fruit is about the size and shape of a large plum, with a tough, usually wrinkled, firm purple skin. Granadillas are larger, with a smooth yellow-orange skin and a lesser flavour. The flesh is orange-yellow with touches of red and a large number of small black and edible seeds. The flavour is not easily described, but it is sweet, strong and full, with a slight sharpness which always dominates in any 'exotic' or 'tropical' fruit juice.

The fruit itself is a good source of Vitamin C and some of the B vitamins. The flower and the leaves are more widely used in folk medicine, as sedatives and for nervous complaints. Passiflora teas and extracts are well known to calm the nerves.

To eat, simply cut the top off the fruit, or cut in half and spoon out the delicious flesh. The flesh can be strained of its seeds for use in soufflés, fools, mousses, icecreams or juices – even one fruit alone can add significant flavour to any mixture. Passion fruits can be made into a jelly, are traditional in Caribbean rum punches, and a classic filling for pavlova (see page 25).

PASSION FRUIT ICECREAM

A wonderfully rich but sharp icecream which does not need beating while it freezes.

4 passion fruit
2 egg yolks
2 oz (50 g) granulated sugar
3 fl. oz (75 ml) water
½ pint (300 ml) double cream

Halve three passion fruit, spoon out the flesh and push through a nylon sieve into a bowl. Discard the seeds.

Place the egg yolks in a bowl and beat. Heat the sugar and water together in a small heavy pan until the sugar dissolves, stirring continuously. Bring to the boil and boil until it reaches the thread stage (225°F/107°C) on a sugar thermometer – or until a little syrup falling from a spoon on to a plate forms a fine thin thread. Pour the hot syrup on to the egg yolks, a little at a time, and beat continuously until the mixture is thick and creamy. Leave to cool.

Stir the passion fruit juices and pulp into the cooled egg mixture. Whip the cream until firm and fold in. Place the icecream in a freezer container and freeze until firm. Serve decorated with the remaining fruit.

Serves 6–8

Papaya or Pawpaw
Carica papaya

Native to Central America, this fast-growing cross between a tall shrub and a tree is now grown all around the tropics and sub-tropics, its large fruit hanging in a bunch from the stalk like a display of, as Waverley Root says, 'not quite fully inflated Rugby balls'. First domesticated by the Carib Indians (from whose language comes the name) it has become one of the most important food plants of the world as it fruits in its first year, although the plant only lasts for about four years. The trees bear either male or female flowers, and in cultivation one male is planted per 20–50 females.

There are several kinds of papaya, among them the five-sided babaco and the papino, a South African hybrid. There are a variety of names: *mamao* (Brazil), *lechoso* (Venezuela) and *fruta bomba* (Cuba, where the word 'papaya' is less than polite). Supplies to the UK all year round come from the Bahamas, Brazil, the Canary Islands, Hawaii, Kenya, Malaysia, Mexico and the West Indies.

The fruits vary in size but are usually about 8 inches (20 cm) long and about 1 lb (450 g) in weight. They are pear or melon shaped with inedible green-yellow-orange skins. Fruit are ripe when soft to the squeeze. The flesh is firm and melon-like in look and texture, and the colour ranges from orange to a deep pink. In the centre is an elongated pouch containing jelly-covered black seeds which glisten like large caviar. The flavour is often slightly sickly at first, but is sweet, delicately perfumed and has been compared to a melange of apricots, melon and ginger.

The fruit contains good amounts of Vitamin A and C. It is said to heal diseases of the gall bladder and liver, and it is particularly associated with digestion because all parts of the plant contain the enzyme papain, a vegetable pepsin, which digests protein. Extracted as a latex (also used in chewing gum manufacture), papain is powdered for use in commercial meat tenderisers. A few drops of papaya juice can tenderize the toughest meats, and in its countries of origin meat is often wrapped and cooked in the leaves. Some puréed flesh, or the inner empty skin, can be applied to the face for a 'tenderising' and beautifying mask. And in 1977, the protein-dissolving powers of papaya were used to cure a post-operative infection in a London kidney transplant patient. The seeds of papaya are also considered good for digestion and are chewed or used as a spice (they taste of mustard and cress); they are reputed to cure worms and, in India, to cause miscarriage.

Papaya is most commonly served halved and seeded for breakfast, sprinkled with lime juice.

Puréed, the flesh is a good base for mousses, fools, icecreams and juices. Papaya can be used similarly to melon – in fruit salads or with Parma ham – and, unripe, it can be cooked as a vegetable, stuffed, accompanied by a sauce, or made into chutney.

GREEN PAPAYA CHUTNEY

This West Indian chutney can also be made with hard green mangoes. Serve with curries.

2 lb (900 g) unripe papayas (or hard, green mangoes)
1 lb (450 g) light soft brown sugar
¾ pint (450 ml) malt vinegar
8 oz (225 g) sultanas, coarsely chopped
2 oz (50 g) fresh root ginger, peeled and finely chopped
2 large garlic cloves, peeled and finely chopped
salt to taste

Peel the papayas (or mangoes) and chop flesh into 1 inch (2.5 cm) cubes. Put into a heavy saucepan, along with all the other ingredients, and simmer gently, stirring occasionally, for about 30 minutes. The mixture should have thickened. Cool briefly, then pour into clean jars and seal. Store in a cool dark place.

Makes about 3 lb/1.4 kg

PERSIMMON
Diospyros kaki

There are several varieties of persimmon: *D. kaki*, also known as kaki and date plum, originated in Japan and China; a North American variety (*D. virginiana*) was introduced to the early settlers by the Indians ('persimmon' comes from a word in an Algonquin language); and a new strain of persimmon was developed by the Israelis in the Sharon Valley, hence its name of sharon fruit.

The persimmon tree is a member of the Ebenaceae family, of which several species yield ebony, that hard wood used for piano keys and chessmen. The trees are hardy, the fruit ripening much later than most other tree fruits; in China they often leave persimmons to freeze on the bare leafless branches when 'the orange or scarlet fruit stand out against the winter landscape like lights on the tree' (Tom Sombart). Main supplies to the UK in winter come from Italy, Israel and, occasionally, Brazil.

The fruit looks like an orange-red apple with a

green-brown calyx. The kaki must only be eaten when it is very ripe – soft with a translucency to the skin (which is inedible, as are the seeds) – as the tannin content makes it extraordinarily astringent. The sharon fruit, however, can be eaten skin and all while firm, is non-astringent and lacks seeds, although there is a pretty residual pattern. The flesh is bright orange and the flavour is sweet.

Sharon fruit are said to contain only 80 calories per 3½ oz (100 g) weight, and to be full of vitamins. The pulp of a soft ripe fruit is close to the normal acid quality of the skin, so could be used for a conditioning facial mask.

Sharon fruit may be eaten just like apples, or sliced to use in winter fruit salads or as garnish for cheesecakes. Alternating with slices of avocado, they make a colourful starter. Kaki can simply be spooned out of the skin and eaten, or can be used in mousses, purée sauces, icecreams, fools or jellies. The pulp can be cooked for use in cakes and pies – an early usage by American settlers who also made beer with pumpkins, persimmons and maple sugar.

PINEAPPLE
Ananas comosus

The pineapple is native to eastern South America and the West Indies, and Columbus first encountered it in 1493. The fruit's resemblance to a pine cone gave it the Spanish name *pina*; the 'apple' came much later, when pineapple growing became a passion of English hot-house gardeners in the 18th century. It had, however, long been known and popular: Charles II is recorded in oils looking askance at the first pineapple produced by his gardener (appropriately named Mr Rose). Despite these early laborious enthusiasms – and successes – pineapples now come to us all year round from South Africa, Kenya, the Ivory Coast, Ghana and Brazil.

The pineapple belongs to the massive Bromeliaceae family, which is among the most versatile of the whole plant kingdom. Its members can grow in almost any kind of habitat, high in trees (called air plants because they seem to take no other nourishment), even on telephone wires! The pineapple itself, however, is firmly terrestrial, growing in cultivation in the centre of a rosette of spiky leaves, no more than 3 feet (90 cm) high. The pineapple is a collective fruit: it develops from many flowers rather than just one, as with most other fruits, and the 100–200 berry-like fruitlets are joined to the core which is a continuation of the stem. In cultivation it bears no seeds, so has to be propagated vegetatively, in much the same way as we produce pot plants. To do this, twist the crown of leaves off the fruit and put them in water or soil so that roots form.

Choose pineapples that have fresh, lively and stiff plumes of leaves. If a bottom leaf pulls out easily, the fruit smells of pineapple, and the flesh is slightly soft, it is ripe. Unripe fruit will not ripen off the plant. Avoid over-ripe or blemished fruit.

Pineapples contain Vitamin C and a digestive enzyme, bromelin. For this reason, pineapples are thought to be an ideal dessert, although they are said to be appetite stimulators as well. The enzyme prevents pineapple being made into a gelatine jelly, so use agar agar, as with kiwifruit, or simmer the fruit gently first to inactivate the enzyme.

Fresh pineapple or its juice can be used in face masks, and hand and feet soaks to soften the skin.

Pineapples can be cut decoratively to serve as desserts by themselves or with other ingredients. Fill the scooped out shell with savoury or sweet mixtures, fruit salad or icecream. Slice in quarters, and prepare as for melon, or peel and slice into classic rings. Take core out if you like. Use chunks or slices with fish, in meat curries, with pork or gammon, in Chinese stir-fry dishes, in savoury salads, in fritters, in flans or upside-down cakes. Pineapple can also be bottled, crystallised and made into marmalade.

PORK CHOPS WITH PINEAPPLE

This is an interesting variation on the grilled gammon and pineapple theme.

4 lean spare-rib pork chops, trimmed
1/2 pineapple, peeled and sliced
1 teaspoon English mustard
2 tablespoons soy sauce
1 tablespoon Worcestershire sauce
1 tablespoon tomato purée
3 tablespoons clear honey
1 tablespoon lime juice
2 tablespoons vegetable oil

Place the chops in a single layer in an ovenproof dish. Cut each pineapple slice into 4 triangles and arrange these on top of the chops. Mix all the remaining ingredients together, pour over the chops, then leave to marinate for 30 minutes.

Preheat the oven to 350°F/180°C/Gas 4 and bake the chops for about an hour, basting occasionally.

Serves 4

POMEGRANATE
Punica granatum

The pomegranate, thought to have originated in Persia, is another ancient fruit. Carbonised Bronze Age remains have been found in a tomb at Jericho. The trees were cultivated in Ancient Egypt and the Bible includes many references; the pomegranate, not the apple, is widely believed to be the fruit of the Tree of Knowledge.

The most famous pomegranate myth is that of Persephone, daughter of Demeter, the goddess of the harvest, who was kidnapped to the underworld by Pluto, the god of the dead, and forced to remain there for six months of every year because she had eaten six pomegranate seeds. According to the myth, this tragedy is what gave rise to the four seasons. Every year, when Persephone is compelled to go back to Hades, Demeter grieves and her tears make the world cold and barren. Spring, as we know it, only returns when Demeter's sadness is dispelled by Persephone's homecoming.

The pomegranate represented fertility in many ancient cultures because of its cornucopia of seeds. In fact, its name is derived from the Latin for apple of many seeds, *pomum granatum*.

Interestingly, *granatum* gave its name to Granada in Spain, where the fruit was cultivated by the Moors, and also to a small 'seeding' and spreading bomb invented in Italy in the 16th century – the grenade – and to that most British of soldiers, the grenadier, who was originally a grenade thrower.

Now grown in many tropical and sub-tropical areas, pomegranates are available in the UK from September to November from Israel, Spain and Cyprus.

Ripe pomegranates should be unblemished and firm, like pink or red oranges with a calyx at the top. The outer skin or rind is hard and inedible. The inner skin is equally inedible, bright yellow in colour, and divides the multi-seeded flesh into compartments. Each seed is golden and sits at the centre of a deep pink gleaming jelly, both of which can be eaten. The flavour can vary from sour to acid-sweet, but is always most refreshing.

To eat pomegranates raw, simply cut in half and spoon out the seeds; these glistening red crystals also make a magnificent garnish or addition to a fruit salad. For juice, put the seeds into a muslin-lined sieve and squeeze or press, taking care not to crush the bitter seeds. In the Middle East pomegranate seeds or juices are used in duck and chicken dishes, in sour sauces and in a soup; pomegranates there are sourer, so add some lemon or lime juice for a more authentic flavour. Use the juice in sorbets, ices and jelly. The dried seeds of sour pomegranates are an important condiment in India, *anardana*. Grenadine is a French pomegranate and sugar syrup which is the colourful basis of many cocktails.

DUCK WITH WALNUT AND POMEGRANATE

This dish from Iran, where it is called Faisinjan, or Fesenjan, can also be made with chicken or lamb.

1 duck, about 4 lb (1.8 kg), cleaned, wiped and trussed
salt and pepper
1 oz (25 g) butter
1 large onion, finely chopped
6 oz (175 g) walnuts, 4 oz (100 g) ground, the remainder
  coarsely chopped
12 fl. oz (350 ml) fresh pomegranate juice (or syrup from
  Middle Eastern stores)
1 tablespoon lemon or lime juice
3 tablespoons brown sugar
1/4 teaspoon each of ground cinnamon and nutmeg

To serve:
1 oz (25 g) walnuts, coarsely chopped
pomegranate seeds

Season the duck with salt and pepper. Heat half the butter in a large heavy lidded pan and brown the duck on all sides. Remove and drain off the fat.

Heat the remaining butter in the pan and fry the onion until soft. Add the walnuts, the pomegranate and lime juices, sugar and spices and bring to the boil. Reduce the heat and return the duck to the pan. Spoon over the sauce then cover and simmer for 1½–2 hours, or until tender. Baste occasionally. When cooked, lift the duck on to a serving plate, quarter it and keep warm. Take fat off the sauce, taste for seasoning, and bring to the boil. Spoon over the duck, garnish with chopped walnuts and pomegranate seeds, and serve with rice.

Serves 4

POMEGRANATE TONING LOTION

'Village beauties in the district of Shaghnan, North-East Afghanistan, where women are renowned for their beauty, use pomegranate juice. They make this by boiling the peel of the fruit and then using the water as an astringent lotion. They also apply this juice to their breasts and fat areas to firm them up.'
The Natural Beauty Book, Clare Maxwell-Hudson (Macdonald and Jane's, 1976).

PRICKLY PEAR
Opuntia ficus-indica

Also known as the 'Indian' or 'Barbary Fig' or 'Pear', 'Cactus Pear' or 'Tuna Fig', the prickly pear is the fruit of a cactus which originated, it is thought, in tropical South America. Appreciated by the Aztecs, it was brought from the New World by Columbus and has since spread all over the temperate world, becoming a pest in the wild in places like South Africa, India and Australia. For a fruit that is so freely (if dangerously) pluckable in many countries, it is available as an import to the UK from few sources – among them Italy, Cyprus, Brazil and Mexico – during the late summer and early winter months. Fruits are sold from iced water and peeled by a rubber-gloved vendor in Malta and Israel. Interestingly, in Israel prickly pears are known as *sabras*, meaning cactus; the same name is applied to native-born Israelis because they are said to be like the fruit, outwardly prickly and pleasant within!

And prickly is the word, for the roughly pear-shaped, red-green-orange fruits bear bristles and invisible spines which bite deep into the skin. Always wear gloves to handle them. The pulp is a bright orange and fibrous in appearance, dotted with small edible seeds. The flavour is fresh, sweet and melon like.

Prickly pears have some Vitamin C and are said, in excess, to cause constipation.

To peel, spear pears on a fork then top and tail. Cut a slit lengthwise, not too deep, and peel back the skin with the knife blade to reveal the glowing flesh. Serve raw as a dessert fruit, in slices or whole, sprinkled with lemon or lime juice, or in a fruit salad. Slices can be candied or crystallised. They make a good jelly, and can be stewed for a compote. The pulp can be puréed for use as a sauce for ham or in a soufflé, and prickly pears team particularly well with bland cheeses such as mozzarella or ricotta.

QUINCE

Cydonia oblonga

An ancient fruit, and a member of the Rosaceae family, quinces probably originated in western Asia, and were cultivated by both the Greeks and Romans. They were thought to be the golden apples of the Hesperides, and some authorities even think it was a quince with which Eve tempted Adam. Chaucer knew the *coine* (from the French *coing*), and a quince sweetmeat, *cotignac*, was a favourite of Joan of Arc. The Latin name *cydonia* comes from the area known as Cydon in Crete, where many quince orchards flourished. Quinces still grow wild throughout Europe, although some are cultivated, and are occasionally available in spring and late autumn.

As John Parkinson recorded in 1629, the fruit are: 'some greater, others smaller, some round like an Apple, others long like a Peare, of a strong heady sent'. The skin of a ripe quince is a bright yellow with a down which should be rubbed off, and the yellow flesh is hard and acid with many seeds. It has to be cooked, when it turns pink.

In the 17th century, Sir Thomas Browne wrote of the 'stomach's comforter, the pleasing quince', and Culpeper listed many remedies including one from the skin's down which, if boiled, could restore hair to the bald! The cores and pips are laxative, and can be made into a decoction for the mouth and throat.

Quinces may be poached in syrup and used with

other fruits in soufflés, icecreams, apple and pear pies. A little quince adds enormous flavour. Quinces contain good quantities of pectin, so are ideal for jams and jellies (see page 21). Their most famous usage is in the original marmalade (*marmelo* is Portuguese for quince): when the young wife of a Dundee grocer named Keiller was presented with some Seville oranges in 1700, she substituted them for quinces in a preserve recipe, and a great Scottish marmalade company was born. Quinces are also used in meat dishes in the Middle East, and in Moroccan tajines.

QUINCE MOUTHWASH

'The quince has several easy applications in home cosmetic formulations. The first is a mouthwash. Simmer the seeds in a pint of water for a mouthwash that will heal the inside of the mouth. It will keep longer if you add a small amount of sherry or brandy to it . . . Incidentally, without the sherry or brandy this quince water is a home remedy for healing burns.'

An ABC of Natural Beauty, Dian Dincin Buchanan,
(Duckworth, 1976)

RAMBUTAN
Nephelium lappaceum

Rambutans are close relatives of lychees, both belonging to the Sapindaceae family. Rambutans originated in Malaysia, but are now grown in other tropical regions of South-East Asia, in Central America and the Philippines. Small supplies come to the UK from Thailand between June and September and some from Sri Lanka in the early winter months.

The clusters of fruit on the tree look rather like sweet chestnuts, for the rambutan is covered with tendrils and, according to Jane Grigson, 'looks like a small hairy animal if you catch sight of it casually'. In fact, in Malay *rambut* means hairy. The reddish-brown skin is hardish and when cracked off reveals a white flesh which is like the lychee. The single white, fibrous seed is inedible. The flesh is less aromatic than the lychee, and contains less Vitamin C.

To eat, simply peel off the skin, or cut the top half of the skin off so that the flesh sits in the bottom half like an egg in a hairy eggcup. Use the seeded fruit in fruit salads, or with vegetable or chicken salads.

SAPODILLA
Achras sapota

The sapodilla – also known as 'Sapodilla Plum', 'Tree Potato', 'Naseberry' and 'Chiku' – is the fruit of a tree native to South America. The family Sapotaceae contains some 600 species of tropical trees, many of which yield edible fruits, timber and latex. Sapodilla wood carvings have been found in Mayan ruins, and the sap of the tree yields chicle which is used in the manufacture of chewing gum and adhesive plasters. Supplies are occasionally available, all year round, in good supermarkets and ethnic groceries.

The fruit is brown and oval, rather like a potato or smooth kiwifruit. They should be soft, not hard; in fact, many experts say they should be left until almost rotten, like medlars. The granular flesh is reddish-yellow in colour and tastes rich, like very ripe bananas or even brown sugar. The black seeds are inedible, as is the skin.

Peel and slice the fruits and serve as they are or in fruit salads. If too soft to slice, purée to use in creamy puddings. In the West Indies, as they contain some 8–12% sugar, sapodillas are boiled down to a syrup and may be made into jam.

TAMARILLO
Cyphomandra betaceae

The tamarillo, also known as the 'Tree Tomato', is the fruit of a small tree which originally came from Peru but is now grown in several other tropical and sub-tropical countries. New Zealand and Kenya cultivate them commercially, and limited supplies are available from February to October. Although a member of the tomato family, the name tamarillo was coined by New Zealand growers because there is only a superficial resemblance to the tomato.

The fruit is egg-shaped with a red or yellow, tough and inedible skin. The flesh is firm and tomato like, red and yellow with many black edible seeds. The flavour of the red tamarillos is quite acidic, rather savoury; yellow ones are slightly sweeter and are said by some to resemble Cape gooseberries.

Tamarillos contain a fair quantity of Vitamin C, some B and iron.

They may be eaten raw like tomatoes, but should be skinned first. They can be sliced or chopped and used like tomatoes in salads, sandwiches, sauces or stews. A raw purée can top desserts, or be made into icecream. They are also used in preserves.

ACKNOWLEDGEMENTS

Thanks are due to many London embassies, trade commissions, companies and individuals, in particular:
Australian Trade Commission, BCB Ltd, Citrus Company of Jamaica Ltd, Embassies of Brazil, Israel and the Philippines, *Eurofruit*, Food and Wine from France, Fresh Fruit and Vegetable Information Bureau/COLEACP, Malaysian Trade Commission, New Zealand Kiwifruit Information Bureau, J. Sainsbury PLC, Rosemary Stark, Waitrose Limited, and Jamie, who was the master taster!

Books which no-one interested in exotic fruit can live without are:
Jane Grigson's Fruit Book, Penguin, 1983
Queer Gear, Carolyn Heal and Michael Allsop, Century, 1985.